DATE DUE

NOV 1 8 2014	
NOV 1 8 2014	
	PRINTED IN U.S.A.

"I'M A SPOKESMAN FOR *MYSELF*. IT JUST
SO HAPPENS THAT THERE'S A BUNCH OF
PEOPLE THAT ARE CONCERNED WITH WHAT
I HAVE TO SAY. I FIND THAT FRIGHTENING
AT TIMES BECAUSE I'M JUST AS CONFUSED AS
MOST PEOPLE. I DON'T HAVE THE ANSWERS
FOR ANYTHING. I DON'T WANT TO BE A
[EXPLETIVE] SPOKESPERSON."

KURT COBAIN

1967–1994

ABDO
Publishing Company

KURT COBAIN

ALTERNATIVE ROCK
INNOVATOR

BY CHRÖS McDOUGALL

CREDITS

Published by ABDO Publishing Company, PO Box 398166, Minneapolis, MN 55439. Copyright © 2013 by Abdo Consulting Group, Inc. International copyrights reserved in all countries. No part of this book may be reproduced in any form without written permission from the publisher. The Essential Library™ is a trademark and logo of ABDO Publishing Company.

Printed in the United States of America, North Mankato, Minnesota
062012
092012

Editor: Lauren Coss
Series Designer: Becky Daum

Library of Congress Cataloging-in-Publication Data
McDougall, Chros.
  Kurt Cobain : alternative rock innovator / by Chros McDougall.
    p. cm. -- (Lives cut short)
  ISBN 978-1-61783-480-6
  1. Cobain, Kurt, 1967-1994--Juvenile literature. 2. Rock musicians--United States--Biography--Juvenile literature. 3. Nirvana (Musical group)--Juvenile literature. I. Title.
  ML3930.C525M43 2012
  782.42166092--dc23
  [B]
                                    2012001289

TABLE OF CONTENTS

CHAPTER 1	*NEVERMIND*	6
CHAPTER 2	ABERDEEN	16
CHAPTER 3	PUNK ROCKER	26
CHAPTER 4	NIRVANA BEGINS	36
CHAPTER 5	ROCK STAR	48
CHAPTER 6	LOVE AND DRUGS	58
CHAPTER 7	BACK TO BASICS	68
CHAPTER 8	FADING AWAY	78
CHAPTER 9	STILL BURNING	86
TIMELINE		96
QUICK FACTS		100
GLOSSARY		102
ADDITIONAL RESOURCES		104
SOURCE NOTES		106
INDEX		110
ABOUT THE AUTHOR		112

1

NEVERMIND

It began with a simple hook. Then came the quiet verse, followed by the loud, screaming chorus. Nirvana guitarist and lead singer Kurt Cobain had written dozens of songs with the same foundation. But this song, "Smells Like Teen Spirit," would change rock music forever.

Cobain wrote lyrics that often did not have an obvious meaning. But the emotions captured throughout the five minutes and two seconds of "Smells Like Teen Spirit" were undeniable. The music and lyrics reflect a mixture of raw

▶ As the lead singer of Nirvana, Kurt Cobain made a lasting impact on modern music.

anger, confusion, angst, and defiance. Those themes were common throughout Nirvana's music. But what set "Teen Spirit" apart from other alternative rock at the time was that people actually listened. In the early 1990s, a generation of American youth was becoming disillusioned with the world. The feelings conveyed in "Smells Like Teen Spirit" resonated with these listeners. The song became their anthem.

A NEW KIND OF MUSIC

The alternative rock revolution began with the song's release on September 10, 1991. At the time, Nirvana was just a little-known band out of Washington State. It had released one album with an independent record label in 1989. Nirvana's second album, *Nevermind*, in 1991 was the band's first major-label album; "Smells Like Teen Spirit" was the album's first single.

People close to the band had an idea that Nirvana

▲ HAIR METAL PERFORMERS, SUCH AS LEAD SINGER JOE ELLIOT OF DEF LEPPARD, HAD A WILDLY DIFFERENT STYLE THAN GRUNGE PERFORMERS, SUCH AS COBAIN.

might be successful. But the definition of success was modest for a band like Nirvana. The 1980s were famous for a type of rock music known as hair metal. Hair metal bands such as Def Leppard, Mötley Crüe, and Van Halen won over millions of fans with their catchy, pop-flavored metal songs and flamboyant shows. Nirvana's music was from a little-known category of alternative rock known as grunge.

Grunge was the opposite of hair metal. Whereas hair metal was catchy and radio friendly, grunge was distorted and often too raw for mainstream listeners. Hair metal bands were known for their showy and flashily dressed rock stars. Grunge bands were largely made up of regular-looking people who hated the stereotypical, self-centered rock star image. And while hair metal bands were playing to sold-out arenas around the world, grunge was barely known outside the Pacific Northwest.

Nirvana featured three members. Dave Grohl played drums, and Chris Novoselic was on bass. But the 24-year-old Cobain was the creative force behind the band. He also embodied what would soon be widely known as grunge culture. Cobain grew up in a broken home in a town on the

Grunge

Grunge developed during the 1980s in and around Seattle, Washington. Grunge bands such as Soundgarden and Alice in Chains had some success during the late 1980s and early 1990s. However, the music style exploded in popularity with the 1991 releases of *Nevermind* and Pearl Jam's album *Ten*. Those albums ushered grunge into the mainstream and helped several other grunge bands score major record deals.

Grunge music, loosely defined as a mix between heavy metal and punk rock, and grunge musicians represented a new era in the United States. They acted angry, confused, and bored with the world. The shabby-looking outfits worn by grunge musicians—particularly the flannel shirt—became a fashion statement for young people across the United States.

▲ CHRIS NOVOSELIC, *LEFT*, COBAIN, *CENTER*, AND DAVE
GROHL, *RIGHT*, MADE UP THE GRUNGE BAND NIRVANA.

economic decline. His future looked bleak when
he dropped out of high school. Without music,
Cobain appeared destined to a life of drugs and
laziness.

Although his example might have been
extreme, Cobain had a story of hopelessness that
resonated with other young people. With his long

Spokesman for a Generation

Cobain claimed he did not put much effort into his lyrics, usually taking them from his poetry at the last minute. Yet the raw feelings conveyed in *Nevermind*— anger, boredom, confusion, frustration—helped the band to connect powerfully with its audience. Cobain resented the idea that he was considered a spokesman for his generation, but fans could not help but be drawn to him and his music. "Kurt could be really mellow and sweet, and then he would flip and be really intense," Novoselic later said. "That's what a lot of *Nevermind* and Nirvana's music is: Kurt's intensity captured."[3]

blond hair and flannel shirts, Cobain looked more like the average young person than the stars of flashy rock bands. But what truly set Cobain apart was his ability to not only capture those resonating emotions in his music, but to capture them in a way that sounded good on the radio.

CLIMBING THE CHARTS

For Nirvana to be a success, its record company, DGC Records, hoped "Smells Like Teen Spirit" could become a minor hit on the alternative music scene. If it did, then *Nevermind*'s second single, "Come As You Are," might have a chance for some success in the mainstream market. If DGC was lucky, Nirvana might sell a half-million copies of *Nevermind* within a year. That would be a success for a band like Nirvana, even though big pop stars could sell that many records in a matter of days. Nobody anticipated Cobain's chilling voice and radio-friendly grunge would catch on so quickly.

Nirvana released *Nevermind* on September 24, 1991, two weeks after "Smells Like Teen Spirit." Record sales started stronger than DGC expected. Then, on October 14, Music Television (MTV) added the "Smells Like Teen Spirit" music video to its regular video rotation. Nirvana—and the band members' lives—would never be the same.

While MTV later transitioned into showing mostly reality shows, during the early 1990s, MTV's programming centered on music videos. The network was highly influential in mainstream music choices. Soon MTV began playing "Smells Like Teen Spirit" more than ten times per day. After that, Nirvana was no longer an underground band, and grunge was no longer popular in just the Pacific Northwest. More than 500,000 copies of *Nevermind* had been sold by November.

Before long, almost every rock or heavy metal radio station had "Smells Like Teen Spirit" in its regular rotation. DGC had originally created fewer than 50,000 copies of *Nevermind*. Fans bought more than 370,000 copies during the last week of December 1991 alone.

On January 11, 1992, Nirvana played its biggest show yet on *Saturday Night Live*. That same day, *Nevermind* surpassed Michael Jackson's album *Dangerous* to take the Number 1 position on the *Billboard* Top 200 Albums chart. That week, Nirvana joined the Red Hot Chili Peppers and Pearl Jam on a short tour. The three bands would become known as some of the most popular and influential bands of their generation. Even though the Red Hot Chili Peppers were the headliners, Nirvana quickly became the biggest draw.

ROCK ICONS

Within a matter of weeks, Nirvana had grown from a promising underground band to one of the biggest bands in the world. Its rise to fame signaled a cultural shift. On *Nevermind*, Nirvana conveyed how American youth felt about the world, and in doing so, the band helped introduce alternative rock to the mainstream masses.

The band's success was not without burden, though, especially for Cobain. He had struggled throughout his life to balance his appreciation for mainstream catchy music with his attraction to punk rock, which despised the excesses of popular commercial music. With *Nevermind*, Cobain had made it as a musician, but he also had to become a rock star. A Nirvana associate said at the time: "People are treating him like a god, and that pisses him off. . . . They're giving Kurt this elevated sense of importance that he feels he doesn't have or deserve."[4]

Cobain had been naturally shy and somewhat of a social outcast for his entire life. He tried to play off his personal struggles in interviews. But behind the scenes, his new life was beginning to spiral out of control. Nirvana concerts became violent affairs as the band members increasingly used them as an outlet for their anger and frustration with the negative consequences of their newfound fame. Cobain also dealt with his issues by taking dangerous amounts of drugs.

It had been a challenging road for Cobain to achieve this level of fame. The days after *Nevermind* would be no less challenging.

——◆——

Lasting Impact

Nevermind and "Smells Like Teen Spirit" had a major impact on American culture. Years later, the album, song, and music video were still regarded as some of the best ever. In 1999, MTV named "Smells Like Teen Spirit" the third-best music video ever. And in 2003, influential music magazine *Rolling Stone* named *Nevermind* the seventeenth-best album of all time. The magazine also named "Smells Like Teen Spirit" the ninth-best song ever.

2

ABERDEEN

urt Donald Cobain was born to parents Donald and Wendy Cobain in Hoquiam, Washington, on February 20, 1967. Nirvana is often associated with Seattle, Washington, where grunge music was centered during the late 1980s and the early 1990s. However, the band members actually spent very little time living in Seattle. Nirvana's true origins were 110 miles (177 km) southwest of the city in Aberdeen, Washington, where the Cobains moved six months after Kurt's birth.

▶ SEATTLE WAS THE CENTER OF THE GRUNGE MUSIC SCENE.

Aberdeen is a small city that sits on Grays Harbor, which opens to the Pacific Ocean. Approximately 16,000 people lived in Aberdeen when Kurt was growing up. The city had seen better days. The logging industry, which dominated the economy, was employing fewer and fewer workers. The frequent rain and overcast skies made the downcast mood seem worse.

A HAPPY KID

Despite the gloominess of Aberdeen, Kurt had a mostly happy childhood. In 1970, Kurt's sister, Kimberly, was born. Don worked as a mechanic at a local gas station. Wendy stayed home and cared for Kurt and Kimberly. Kurt's parents were able to provide a mostly stable upbringing. Wendy and Kurt had a loving relationship.

Young Kurt was somewhat of a loner, and he could be moody. He spent a lot of time playing with his imaginary friend or pretending he was an alien. At one point, Kurt was fascinated with becoming a stunt daredevil like famous stuntman Evel Knievel. Kurt was also hyperactive. His parents tried various methods to calm him down, including different kinds of drugs. They were finally able to slow him down a bit by removing sugar from his diet.

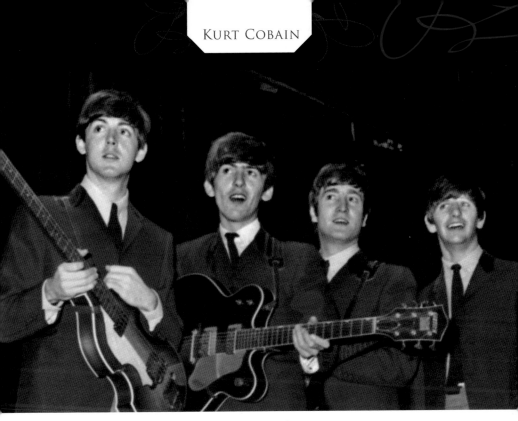

▲ THE BEATLES WERE ONE OF KURT'S FAVORITE BANDS AS A CHILD.

Still, Kurt remained a mostly happy young boy. His family remembers him being a great entertainer. Kurt first took an interest in music at age two. Kurt's aunt Mary was a country musician. She introduced him to popular rock bands such as the Beatles and the Monkees. Mary also gave Kurt his first guitar lessons. The lessons did not last long, as Kurt was too distracted to focus. But Kurt loved the music.

When Kurt was seven, Mary gave him a bass drum. It was the perfect gift. Kurt would strap on the drum and walk up and down the street singing and banging it to the beats of his favorite Beatles and Monkees songs. Wendy said of Kurt,

He got up every day with such joy that there was another day to be had. . . . He was so enthusiastic. He would come running out of his bedroom so excited that there was another day ahead of him and he couldn't wait to find out what it was going to bring him.[1]

EVERYTHING CHANGES

In 1975, just after Kurt's eighth birthday, Wendy filed for divorce from Don. The news sent Kurt's world crashing down. He blamed the split on his own

An Artist

Kurt is best known as a musician, but he also showed great talent as an artist. People first began to take notice of Kurt's art when he was approximately seven years old. He liked drawing and painting, but Kurt was never satisfied with his work. Once, the elementary school newspaper invited Kurt to draw a picture for its front page. It was a big honor, and everybody told Kurt they loved the picture, but he was angry. Kurt hated the drawing, and he could not believe the newspaper would print such a bad picture.

As with his music, Kurt's family members tried to encourage his art. "After a while, it kind of got crammed down his throat," Wendy said. "Every present was a paintbrush or an easel. We kind of almost killed it for him."[2] Kurt never gave up on art, though. He could draw very well, and Kurt's artwork appeared on the Nirvana album covers of both *Incesticide* and *In Utero*. However, he also had an interest in dark or bizarre subjects. For example, he was

failings. Those feelings were
only enhanced as the bitter
legal proceedings stretched on
and on.

The cheerfulness young
Kurt was known for turned
to sourness. He developed a
generally negative attitude,
and he often became angry.
Kurt and Kimberly lived with
Wendy. But Kurt clashed
with Wendy's new boyfriend.
Within a year, he moved
in with his dad in nearby
Montesano, Washington.

Divorce

When Don and Wendy
Cobain divorced in 1975,
they were not alone. US
culture was changing dur-
ing the 1970s, and divorce
rates increased during that
time. The generation Kurt
grew up in was the first in
which it became normal for
kids to have divorced parents. It was a life-changing
experience for Kurt, but
one that made him and his
music more relatable to
fans who had gone through
similar situations.

Things initially got better. Though Kurt had
never been as close with his dad, Don helped
Kurt better understand the divorce. Don also
spent a lot of time with Kurt, spoiling him with
attention and gifts. But any reconciliation was
lost in February 1978 when Don remarried.
According to Kurt, Don once told him he would
never remarry. Kurt felt betrayed. To make
matters worse for young Kurt, Don's new wife
brought a stepson and stepdaughter into the
family.

Kurt's new stepmother tried to reach out to him, but he showed no interest. His attitude grew even worse than it had been before. Kurt began skipping school and ignoring his chores around the house. He also began bullying his new stepsiblings.

The one thing that seemed to keep Kurt's interest during his troubled times was music. Even though options were limited in local record stores and on the small-town radio stations, Kurt appreciated the different music he heard on the radio, from country to folk to blues.

A LONER

Kurt spent a lot of time on his own when he was growing up. As a sensitive, arty kid in a macho, blue-collar, logging town, Kurt was often written off by classmates as being weird. He did not have many friends, and the kids he spent time with tended to be outcasts like him.

Kurt was drawn to a group of marijuana-smoking hard-rock fans for a time. They introduced him to heavy metal bands such as Black Sabbath, Led Zeppelin, and Kiss. Kurt discovered that his dad actually owned several

An Early Poem

Perhaps Kurt's first-ever poem was written on the wall of his bedroom following his parents' divorce. It read: "I hate Mom, I hate Dad / Dad hates Mom, Mom hates Dad / it simply makes you want to be sad."[3]

▲ ALTHOUGH KURT HAD BEEN A MOSTLY HAPPY KID, HE BECAME SULLEN AFTER HIS PARENTS' DIVORCE.

hard rock records. Most were unopened when Kurt found them, but Kurt took a lot of interest in them. Don, however, showed little desire to listen to the records with Kurt.

Don had grown frustrated with Kurt's attitude. It seemed no matter what Don and

Anti-Athlete

Don Cobain loved sports, and he desperately wanted his son to share that enthusiasm. Kurt made very little effort to try. While on a baseball team, Kurt intentionally struck out so he could avoid playing. Kurt showed more promise on the junior high wrestling team. He hated the sport and the jocks on the team, but his stubbornness and scrappy fighting style brought him some success. It all ended when Kurt—knowing it would make his father upset—purposely let his opponent pin him in a championship fight. Kurt moved in with relatives soon after.

his new wife tried, Kurt just rejected the family and acted out. Don tried taking a more strict approach to raising Kurt, but Kurt responded by rebelling and making more trouble. Finally Don sent Kurt to live with relatives.

▲ KURT, *SECOND ROW*, WAS ON HIS SCHOOL'S TRACK TEAM IN NINTH GRADE.

3

PUNK ROCKER

For the next five years, Kurt was shuffled between three sets of aunts and uncles as well as Don's parents.

For a time, Kurt lived with Wendy's brother Chuck Fradenburg. It was the perfect place for Kurt. The 13-year-old generally disliked authority, but Fradenburg, who was the drummer in a local rock band, was one of the few adults Kurt respected. Fradenburg offered to get Kurt a guitar or a bike for his fourteenth birthday. Kurt chose guitar, and Chuck bought his nephew a used guitar and amplifier.

▸ KURT EMBRACED PUNK MUSIC AND THE EDGY LIFESTYLE THAT WENT ALONG WITH IT.

KURT COBAIN

▲ KURT, *FRONT LEFT*, PLAYED DRUMS FOR A WHILE, BUT
HE QUICKLY SWITCHED TO GUITAR WHEN HIS UNCLE GAVE
HIM ONE AS A BIRTHDAY GIFT.

Kurt immediately quit the drums and began
obsessing over his new instrument. Before
long, the teenager had taught himself to play
a series of popular songs. They ranged from
the Kingsmen's 1950s classic "Louie Louie"
to AC/DC's heavy metal hit "Back in Black."
Those songs represented Kurt's taste in music

at the time. However, those tastes would soon change drastically.

By ninth grade, marijuana, alcohol, and other drugs were becoming a regular part of Kurt's life. They made him act even more withdrawn and surly around his family and others. Kurt transferred to Aberdeen High School for tenth grade in 1983, and he moved back in with Wendy and her new husband. It was still not a good fit. Kurt immediately clashed with his new stepfather, and he was a pain for the rest of the family too.

PUNK ROCK

With his constant moving, Kurt had little stability and his home life continued to be stressful. However, he made new friends and found a crowd he fit in with. In the summer of 1983, Kurt met Matt Lukin. Matt played bass in a local rock band called the Melvins. Several kids in the local alternative crowd were drawn to the Melvins, and Kurt was one of them. He became a loyal devotee to the band and friends with Matt and the Melvins' singer Buzz Osborne. Through them, Kurt learned a new style of music—and a new lifestyle.

Buzz was the most influential in introducing Kurt to punk rock. The Melvins' front man would make mixtapes for Kurt with the newest punk music. In August 1984, before Kurt's junior year of high school, Buzz took Kurt up to Seattle to see Black Flag, his first punk rock show. According to legend, Kurt sold all of his mainstream records to pay for the trip. But it was worth it. Kurt said he was "instantly converted."[1]

A Rebel and a Reject

Punk rockers considered themselves to be society's rejects and outcasts. They did whatever they wanted and did not care what others thought of them. Kurt identified with the punk attitude and lifestyle. However, the new influences pushed him further away from his family

The Melvins

Buzz Osborne once said: "Without us, there is no Nirvana."[2] Osborne was referring to his band, the Melvins, and few would disagree with his statement. The Melvins were founded in the Aberdeen/Montesano area during the early 1980s. The heavy, growling style of punk rock the Melvins were playing by the mid-1980s is considered some of the first grunge sounds. "Every Seattle band of the late '80s owes a little something to the Melvins—a band that slowed down the tempo and played sludgy riffs," Chris Novoselic wrote in a 2009 blog entry for *Seattle Weekly*.[3]

The Melvins had a particularly large influence on Nirvana. Kurt and Chris were loyal devotees of the band in high school, often hanging around band practices and helping move equipment to gigs. Kurt even tried out to join the band, but he completely froze once his tryout began.

▲ Buzz Osborne, the lead singer of punk rock band the Melvins, taught Cobain about punk culture.

and the rest of mainstream society. Before, Kurt had kept largely to himself. As he grew older, he accepted that he was different from people in Aberdeen and went out of his way to alienate himself even more. Kurt picked fights with classmates and painted offensive graffiti around town. One friend's mother said entertaining Kurt was "like living with the devil."[4]

Kurt's family desperately wanted him to get his life on track. He was naturally inquisitive and an avid reader, but nothing they tried could get him to focus in school. Although he was interested in certain subjects, Kurt did not respect his teachers. Instead of applying himself in the classroom, he often fought with teachers and skipped school.

At one point, Kurt agreed to give up music and to move back in with his dad. The move was promising but short-lived. Upon moving in, Kurt took a navy recruiting test and scored high. Don hoped Kurt might enlist and learn some discipline. Instead, with Don and a recruiter waiting for him, Kurt got high on marijuana in the other room and then walked out. He did not see his father again for eight years.

With a combination of constant moving and a general apathy toward his education, Kurt found himself nearly two years behind in school with just one semester left in his senior year. Some teachers tried to help him make up the

Hometown Hostility

When Kurt was younger, he simply avoided most people in Aberdeen, whom he often referred to as rednecks. Upon embracing the punk lifestyle, Kurt set out to antagonize them. He would often show up at parties uninvited, sometimes putting eggs in the hosts' beds. Kurt also used graffiti to challenge people's conservative values, writing highly offensive statements around Aberdeen. Kurt was once arrested for graffiti and had to pay a $180 fine.

credits. Instead, Kurt dropped out just a few weeks shy of what would have been his 1985 graduation.

ON HIS OWN

After dropping out of school, Cobain moved back in with Wendy, but the clashes continued. Wendy wanted her son to get a job and learn to take care of himself. Cobain had decided his future was in music, and that would be his job. Frustrated, Wendy kicked Cobain out that same summer. Cobain moved into an apartment with a friend and took on a series of low-paying jobs. The little money Cobain earned went mostly to supporting his increasing drug and alcohol habits. By December, he was back on the street.

Cobain spent his days at the library, reading books or scribbling poems and drawings into notebooks. At night, Cobain slept on friends' couches, in their vans, and even outside for a brief period. A former teacher took Cobain in for a short time, but that soon ended on a sour note.

Homosexuality

Kurt and classmate Myer Loftin became close friends when Myer announced he was gay. Homosexuals were rare in Aberdeen, and many people were not accepting of the lifestyle. Kurt stuck with his friend, and soon people believed he, too, was gay. At first, Kurt liked that people thought he was different from them. "I started being proud of the fact that I was gay even though I wasn't," Kurt said.[5] However, when other students beat Kurt up, he decided to end his friendship with Myer. Still, Kurt remained a supporter of gay rights throughout his life.

Eventually, Cobain ended up living with Lukin in a grimy shack near Wendy's house.

Cobain's artwork was growing increasingly odd. He had a particular infatuation with dolls, leaving them hung by their necks from his ceiling. And his drug problems continued getting worse. By this point, Cobain had taken just about every drug available to him. His life seemed lazy, drug filled, and without much hope for the future. It was not a lifestyle that predicted success in the music industry, yet it was at this time that Kurt's music career was finally gaining some momentum.

FINALLY, A BAND

Cobain had been writing music for years, but he was never able to find people to play with. In 1986, he formed Fecal Matter, his first band. Fecal Matter and his next band, Brown Towel, gave some raw previews of the sounds Cobain would create with Nirvana. But none of Cobain's early bands were ever truly established. He could never find bandmates who were good enough and who shared his vision, so the early bands constantly changed names and members and broke up.

There was one local musician who Cobain had his eye on. Cobain had seen Chris Novoselic

▲ CHRIS NOVOSELIC WENT TO HIGH SCHOOL WITH COBAIN. HE WOULD BE A FOUNDING MEMBER OF THE BAND THAT BECAME NIRVANA.

at Aberdeen High School and while spending time with the Melvins. He knew Novoselic was a talented musician. Cobain recruited Novoselic to join him in 1986. They briefly formed the Sellouts, a cover band that played the music of Creedence Clearwater Revival with Kurt playing drums. In late 1987, Cobain and Novoselic teamed up with drummer Aaron Burckhard. They continued experimenting with names, but their momentum finally began picking up. This time, Cobain was the lead singer.

4

Nirvana Begins

Cobain's first successful band brought positive changes to his life. Cobain and Novoselic quickly became good friends. Together they would drive 50 miles (80.5 km) to Olympia, Washington, where an underground music scene was thriving. Cobain also began dating a woman in Olympia, Tracy Marander.

In Aberdeen, Cobain found focus in his daily life in the form of his new band. Cobain and Novoselic clicked as partners. Burckhard did not fit in quite as well, but at least he could play.

▶ COBAIN'S BAND, STILL WITHOUT ITS FINAL NAME, WAS ON THE BRINK OF SUCCESS.

36

KURT COBAIN

With a competent band for the first time, Cobain was intent on making it work.

Cobain might have had lazy tendencies toward other aspects of his life, but he was a perfectionist when it came to his music. He got Novoselic to buy into his newfound drive, and the band's rehearsals soon became intense sessions lasting long into the night. Their hard work began paying off. In March, the band—still without an official name—got its first gig. The group's early shows were small and unpredictable. Usually it would perform at local house parties. The band members often showed up drunk or high on drugs, and their behavior was erratic.

Still, the band's early music gave some hints of what was to come. Some of its earliest songs, such as "Love Buzz" and "Floyd the Barber," would land on Nirvana's first album. But few who watched these three unusual musicians early on could have predicted the band's bright future.

Sickness

Cobain suffered from chronic bronchitis in his early years, followed by scoliosis as a teen. However, Cobain's most debilitating sickness came in the form of a sharp, piercing stomach pain he began experiencing shortly after moving to Olympia. It eventually got to the point where he said the pain "made me want to kill myself every day."[1] The source of the pain remained a mystery for many years. Cobain blamed it for his later addictions to heroin and opiates, claiming he took the drugs largely because they dulled the pain. In 1993, a doctor diagnosed it as a pinched nerve in his spine, and he was able to treat the condition.

THE DEMO TAPE

In May 1987, Cobain moved in with Marander in Olympia. It was a risky move. One month earlier, the band had experienced a minor breakthrough when it played on KAOS, a college radio station in Olympia. But with Cobain's move and Novoselic's later move to Tacoma, Washington— another 30 miles (48 km) east of Olympia—the trio was suddenly separated.

The era that followed was marked by long commutes to meet up for rehearsals. At one point, Cobain traveled more than 400 miles (644 km) round trip to get everyone to and from band practice. That routine meshed well with Cobain's lifestyle in Olympia. Marander worked the overnight shift at a cafeteria during the time when the band usually practiced. When Cobain woke up around noon, he spent most of his day playing guitar, working on art projects, or watching television. He rarely left his tiny apartment, which was filled with pets

Tracy Marander

Osborne introduced Cobain to Tracy Marander in 1986. She soon became Cobain's first serious girlfriend. Marander, also a punk rock fan, supported Cobain during the early years of Nirvana. However, she eventually got tired of his laziness around the house and lack of income. They split up in 1990 after three years of dating. In response, Cobain sang the lyrics "I can't see you every night for free" on *Bleach* in the song "About a Girl," which he wrote about Marander.[2]

including cats, rabbits, rats, and turtles. Usually Cobain left only to go to band practices or parties.

The band dropped Burckhard that fall and began temporarily working with the Melvins' talented drummer, Dale Crover. With the new drummer, Cobain was ready for the band to take the next step. When Cobain finally got a job as a janitor, music was his motivation. By January 1988, he had saved up enough money to buy time at a recording studio in Seattle.

With the help of up-and-coming producer Jack Endino, the band recorded ten songs. Endino had never heard of Cobain

Chris Novoselic

At six foot seven and with a goofy personality, Chris Novoselic was hard to miss. He was born in California in 1965 to Croatian immigrants. His family moved to Aberdeen when he was 14 years old. Like Cobain, Novoselic was an outsider among the blue-collar types in Aberdeen. And also like Cobain, Novoselic abused drugs and alcohol. However, Novoselic was able to curb his habits once Nirvana made it big.

Novoselic, who now goes by Krist Novoselic, his given name, was one of Cobain's closest friends. In Nirvana, he was known for his outrageous stunts and humor. "Krist was one of the only people who could make Kurt laugh," Nirvana drummer Dave Grohl said later. "They shared a sense of humor. Krist could make Kurt start laughing, rolling, and crying on the floor."[3] Novoselic was known for his interest in politics. After Nirvana, he transitioned his attention toward

▲ PRODUCER JACK ENDINO SAW POTENTIAL IN COBAIN
AND HIS BAND'S MUSIC.

before working on the band's demo. But he left
the recording session impressed, especially with
Cobain's powerful voice. Three of the songs
would end up on Nirvana's 1989 album *Bleach*.
Four showed up on 1992's *Incesticide*.

The demo marked the beginning of a proud
era in Cobain's music career. For the first time, he
felt like a legitimate musician. As he celebrated
his twenty-first birthday that February, the future
looked bright. The band's following continued
slowly growing within Washington. The band

was written up in a local music magazine and began playing shows in small bars and clubs. Meanwhile, Endino sent the band's demo tape to independent record labels across the United States. Endino had also passed the demo to one of the cofounders of Sub Pop, a fledgling local label.

Sub Pop had begun just a year earlier, in 1987. Yet it was already earning a reputation for discovering hot new bands in the Pacific Northwest. When Sub Pop approached the group about joining the label, Cobain and his bandmates agreed to the partnership.

Sub Pop

During the late 1980s, the independent record label Sub Pop played a major role in establishing the grunge phenomenon in the Pacific Northwest. The label, founded by Bruce Pavitt and Jonathan Poneman, is credited with discovering several up-and-coming bands, including Mudhoney, Nirvana, and Soundgarden. Although Nirvana left the label before breaking through with *Nevermind*, Sub Pop still received a small percentage of the album's sales. Pavitt later said the label might have gone out of business had it not been for that money.

Becoming Nirvana

Cobain and Novoselic's band went by several different names during its early days. Among them were Skid Row, Ted Ed Fred, Bliss, Throat Oyster, Pen Cap Chew, and Windowpane. Around 1988, it finally settled on Nirvana. The name comes from a Hindu and Buddhist state of enlightenment, which Cobain interpreted to mean "total peace after death."[4]

▲ Bruce Pavitt, *LEFT*, and Jonathan Poneman, *RIGHT*, founded Sub Pop Records, the label that launched Cobain's band.

Finding a regular drummer took even longer than finding a name. Crover left to rejoin the Melvins shortly after recording the demo. Another drummer from Aberdeen lasted only a few months. The band even brought Burckhard back briefly. Then, in May 1988, Chad Channing took over.

With a new drummer and a minor record deal, Nirvana took its next steps. Its first single, "Love Buzz," was released in November. Cobain was hesitant to use the song as the group's first single because it was a cover. A Dutch band had written the song in the 1960s. However, he eventually agreed it would be a good debut. "Love Buzz" had the classic Nirvana mix between a catchy pop song and a screaming, distorted mess.

Nirvana was hardly a major band at the time, but it was making a name for itself in the growing underground Seattle music scene. Cobain was conflicted about fame, but he often said his goal was simply for Nirvana to become a respected alternative rock band. The band seemed well on its way.

In a letter to his grandparents around Christmas 1988, Cobain wrote, "I'm happier than I ever have been."[5] That feeling grew a few weeks later when Nirvana went back to the studio to record its first full album, *Bleach*. It was named after signs the band saw while on the road. The signs encouraged drug users to clean their needles with bleach to prevent the spread of HIV.

Bleach came out in the summer of 1989. The music had hints of the strong melodies that would later make *Nevermind* a mainstream success. Cobain's versatile vocals especially stood out. However, Cobain later lamented that the band focused more on making a stereotypical grunge album than a unique Nirvana album. Alternative music critics were similarly conflicted. Some saw great potential in the music while others saw nothing out of the ordinary.

Nonetheless, Nirvana now had a full-length album, and the band soon embarked on its first US tour. It was not glamorous. Nirvana played mostly bars, and the band members often had to sleep in their van between shows. But they were finally making it as musicians. "We were totally poor," Cobain said, "but, God, we were seeing the United States for the first time. And we were in a band and we were making just enough money to survive. It was awesome."[6]

The band briefly experimented with a second guitarist on that 26-stop US tour. However, it was back to a trio when it left for a European tour

▲ THE BAND BECAME KNOWN FOR THEIR ERRATIC AND
DESTRUCTIVE BEHAVIOR DURING PERFORMANCES.

later that year. Attendance at the shows picked up
as the European tour went on. And, after a slow
start, sales of *Bleach* picked up as well.

MOUNTING TENSION

Tensions mounted as Nirvana and fellow
grunge band Tad traveled around Europe.
Cobain had stopped smoking cigarettes and
marijuana to protect his vocal chords. But
others openly smoked in the cramped van,
increasing his anxiety.

As the tour went on, Cobain and Novoselic became increasingly frustrated with Channing. The Nirvana originals had a clear idea of the sound they wanted from the drums. They felt they were not getting that sound from Channing. The frustrated band members lashed out. At one show in Rome, Italy, Cobain had a nervous breakdown and threatened to jump off a stack of amplifiers.

The European tour had largely been a success. Fans there were enthusiastic and filled Nirvana's audiences. The English music publications reacted positively to Nirvana. But even more changes were in store for the band from Aberdeen.

5

ROCK STAR

After another short US tour, Cobain and Novoselic parted ways with Channing. They wanted a harder-hitting drummer. As a former drummer himself, Cobain was especially picky. After a few trials with other drummers, Nirvana found Dave Grohl. Grohl moved to Washington State in September 1990, becoming the band's permanent drummer. Cobain called Grohl "the drummer of our dreams."[1]

Meanwhile, Nirvana's relationship with Sub Pop was fraying. The label was struggling

▶ IN DAVE GROHL, *CENTER*, COBAIN AND NOVOSELIC FINALLY FOUND A DRUMMER THEY COULD STICK WITH.

financially, and the Nirvana members felt Sub Pop was not giving the band enough support and disagreed with the label's marketing strategies.

At the same time, Nirvana had developed a legitimate buzz in underground music circles. Some mainstream record labels were approaching the band about signing on. No bands that sounded like Nirvana had gained mainstream commercial success, but the band decided a major label was the best next step.

Nirvana's members met with various labels from California to New York. Eventually, in the winter of 1991, they signed with DGC Records. With the trio set and a new record contract, the band headed to Van Nuys, California, during the summer of 1991 to create *Nevermind*. On this album, Cobain was ready to try new things.

The Pixies were one of Cobain's favorite alternative bands, and he liked the way the group incorporated catchy

Dave Grohl

Cobain and Novoselic could always find something wrong with their drummers, whether it was a bad taste in music or simply not hitting the drums hard enough. They had none of those problems with Dave Grohl. The drummer, who grew up in Virginia, always had a love of music. And like Cobain and Novoselic, his musical tastes eventually turned to punk rock. Grohl played in the hard-core punk band Scream before joining Nirvana. Although he was never given much creative control in Nirvana, Grohl was a talented all-around musician. After Nirvana, he created the Foo Fighters, for which he is the lead singer and a guitarist.

pop sounds into its music. He wanted Nirvana to do the same. Yet at the same time, Cobain did not want to abandon Nirvana's heavy and intense sound. Producer Butch Vig would help the band get the sound Cobain wanted.

Most punk rock and early alternative rock albums featured very simple recording. The sound quality was intentionally bad, and the albums were meant to sound like live performances. Vig brought a more mainstream approach to recording alternative and punk rock, creating a more polished sound.

Vig had recorded seven songs with Nirvana for a demo while the group was still with Sub Pop. Several of those songs were early versions of songs that would later appear on *Nevermind*. The young band impressed Vig. He could tell the new songs would have more mainstream appeal than those on *Bleach*.

The *Nevermind* recording sessions were intense, especially for Cobain. He was in the studio for long hours working on his various contributions to the album, including guitar, vocals, and even finishing writing the lyrics to some songs. Sometimes Cobain sang so hard he damaged his voice. He was only able to do one or two takes of a song per day. But as the summer continued, a buzz began developing around the recordings. Some people had heard Nirvana's previous recordings with Vig. Word began spreading that *Nevermind* would be even better than Nirvana's previous work.

LIFE IS GOOD

Nirvana wrapped up recording on *Nevermind* in mid-June. It would be approximately three months before the album was released. As Cobain later said,

> *The best times were right when* Nevermind *was coming out and we went on that American tour where we were playing clubs. . . . There was this massive feeling in the air, this vibe of energy. Something really special was happening.*[2]

The band set out on a short tour, playing clubs on the West Coast. Then it joined Sonic Youth—a band the members of Nirvana looked up to—on a tour of outdoor European festivals. Playing with Sonic Youth was a dream for Cobain, and he later said Sonic Youth's level of success would have been ideal for Nirvana.

Cobain had reason to believe Nirvana could be at that level. He knew *Nevermind* was going to be a good album. Just before *Nevermind* was released on September 24, 1991, Nirvana began another North American club tour, this time as headliners. Few could have guessed how much further the band would rise.

SMELLS LIKE CHANGES

Everything began changing as "Smells Like Teen Spirit," the first single off *Nevermind*, began climbing up the charts. In October, *Nevermind* reached gold status, meaning a half-million records had been sold. In January, *Rolling Stone* called Nirvana "the world's first triple-platinum punk-rock band."[3] That meant *Nevermind* had sold more than 3 million copies. Before then, only a few alternative rock bands had reached a mainstream audience. But none shattered the rock-and-roll establishment in the way that Nirvana did in 1991.

It took some time for the band's mainstream success to sink in. Nirvana was feverishly touring in Europe that fall. Its members had little idea that "Smells Like Teen Spirit" was being played over and over again on MTV and radio stations of all genres. They knew it was a good song, but

▲ RELEASED IN 1991, *NEVERMIND* MADE NIRVANA'S BRAND OF GRUNGE MUSIC MAINSTREAM.

they never expected it to become such a crossover success.

The reality was that *Nevermind* had become a barrier-breaking album. Cobain's songwriting drew in both the disenchanted teenagers of the grunge scene and the mainstream audiences that simply appreciated a good song. Alternative rock—and specifically grunge—was quickly replacing hair metal as the rock music of choice for many people, and that was in large part due to Nirvana.

While the commercial success was a dream for DGC, it was bittersweet for Nirvana. As *Nevermind* crossed over into other genres, Nirvana found its fans becoming less and less alternative. Publicly Cobain maintained he was fine with the mainstream success. "It really isn't affecting me as much as it seems like it is in interviews and the way that a lot of journalists have portrayed my attitude," he told *Rolling Stone* in April 1992. "I'm pretty relaxed with it."[5]

A different story played out behind the scenes. Rumors began spreading that Nirvana had become too popular and might break up. Meanwhile, the band's destructive tendencies increased as the band's members became more frustrated with their growing—and changing—fan base.

Nirvana audiences began to resemble the kind of people Cobain and Nirvana did not want to attract—the jocks, the metal heads, the macho guys from Aberdeen. Cobain considered those people to be closed-minded. Just as he had done with people in Aberdeen growing up, Cobain made an effort to alienate himself from Nirvana's new fans. The trio often showed up for concerts drunk and unruly. They more frequently and more deliberately sabotaged their shows by destroying their equipment. Afterward, they destroyed their dressing room and anything else they felt like wrecking at the time. "I found myself being overly obnoxious during the *Nevermind* tour, because I noticed that there were more average people coming into our shows and I didn't want them there," Cobain said. "They started to get on my nerves."[6]

The hectic touring schedule and the band's increasing drug and alcohol use forced Nirvana to cancel the rest of its European tour in early December. Nirvana's popularity was just beginning to take off, though. By January 1992, a little more than three months after its release, *Nevermind* was Number 1 on the

Life on the Road

Touring with Nirvana in mid-to-late 1991 was almost always chaotic. One associate described Nirvana's tours as "twenty-three hours of sheer boredom, and one hour of sheer terror."[7]

Cobain and his bandmates were unpredictable, both on and off the stage. They drank heavily and took drugs, which only enhanced their unpredictability. Cobain sometimes wore dresses on stage. The band members crowd surfed, spit, and argued with bouncers. They were not afraid to create general chaos among the fans. Also, the band was almost certain to trash its instruments and dressing room after it was finished playing. Cobain was known to be shy, but he was a notorious troublemaker on tours. "Everything you fix, a guy like Kurt goes and deliberately unfixes it because he's a cutie pie, you know?" said Nirva-

▲ AS THEIR MUSIC BECAME MORE POPULAR WITH
MAINSTREAM AUDIENCES, THE MEMBERS OF NIRVANA
LASHED OUT DURING CONCERTS.

music charts and Nirvana was performing on
Saturday Night Live. And things were picking up
in Cobain's personal life as well.

———◆———

6

LOVE AND DRUGS

*C*obain first met Courtney Love at a Nirvana show in 1989. She was the singer and guitarist in her own alternative rock band, Hole, and she was exactly what Cobain was looking for in a woman. "She looked like a classic punk rock chick," Cobain remembered.[1] Love acted like a classic punk rocker too. She was loud, unpredictable, and abrasive. The second time she saw Cobain, at a concert in May 1991, she greeted him by punching him in the gut. He punched her back, and they began wrestling.

▶ COBAIN FOUND A SOMETIMES-VOLATILE ROMANCE WITH COURTNEY LOVE.

Their attraction toward each other grew from there, and they soon started dating.

During tours that could sometimes get boring in between shows, Cobain found excitement just by being around Love. "If I just happened to walk down the street with her, someone might attack us with a knife for no reason," he said, "just because she seems like the kind of person that attracts things like that."[2]

To outsiders, Cobain and Love's relationship appeared dysfunctional. Love was a strong-willed woman and seemed to dominate her submissive boyfriend. But it was a relationship that seemed to work for both of them.

Drugs had been a regular part of

Courtney Love

Courtney Love was born Courtney Michelle Harrison in 1964 in San Francisco, California. Following her parents' divorce when she was five, Love moved from place to place around the world, living everywhere from Oregon to New Zealand. Growing up, Love was known for her outrageous and shocking personality. As a teenager, she even worked as a stripper for a time.

During the 1980s, Love became interested in music and acting. She appeared in a few movies during her career but found the most success as a musician. After short stints in other bands, Love founded Hole in 1989. Love did not shy away from attention like Cobain, and there was some animosity between the couple when he became a famous rock star. Although Hole's first album was well received, it was not until she married Cobain that Love and Hole really took off.

▲ COURTNEY LOVE, *CENTER RIGHT*, WAS THE LEAD SINGER OF THE ALTERNATIVE BAND HOLE.

Cobain's life long before meeting Love, but with her, Cobain's habit got worse. He had begun taking heroin again in 1990. For years, Cobain maintained that his heroin habit was simply a means of temporarily relieving his stomach pain. Without it, he said, he felt suicidal. So, after a break, he started taking it again with Love in the fall of 1991. This time, they both became addicted.

A HEROIN JUNKIE

As *Nevermind* rapidly climbed up the charts in late 1991, some close to Cobain began to worry about his heroin habit. He looked frail and sickly while on a short December 1991 tour with the Red Hot Chili Peppers and Pearl Jam. In January 1992, a journalist from *BAM* magazine alluded to the fact that Cobain looked and acted like he was on heroin.

Those concerns became considerably more serious just before Nirvana's *Saturday Night Live* performance and *Nevermind*'s move to Number 1. That was when Love discovered she was pregnant with Cobain's child. Cobain and Love visited a doctor once they discovered Love was pregnant. The doctor said their baby would likely be healthy if Love immediately stopped using drugs. According to Love, she immediately quit heroin.

On February 24, 1992, two months after learning Love was pregnant, the couple married. The wedding was in Hawaii, following Nirvana's first tour of Asia and

Heroin

Heroin is a highly addictive drug that affects brain function and is often injected directly into the bloodstream. Users experience an initial rush of exhilaration before a sense of drowsiness sets in. The drug affects the brain's ability to complete basic functions such as breathing, and overdosing on heroin can be fatal. Regular users who stop taking the drug can experience painful withdrawal periods.

Australia. It was a small ceremony and one very fitting for the couple—Cobain wore pajamas. Whether or not Love had truly given up heroin at the time was not certain. However, Cobain was high on the drug at the wedding.

Even though Love claimed she had stopped using drugs, tension grew between the band members. Novoselic and his wife did not believe Love was off drugs, and they felt it was wrong for Cobain and Love to be using drugs while Love was pregnant. Because of the tension, Novoselic and his wife were not invited to the wedding.

Cobain struggled to stay off drugs during Love's pregnancy. At home, he would sneak away from Love to take heroin so she would not be tempted to join him. Cobain also made efforts to hide his drug use from the public. In April 1992, he told *Rolling Stone* he no longer took drugs or drank because he was too sick.

"All drugs are a waste of time," Cobain said. "They destroy your memory and your self-respect and everything that goes along with your self-esteem. . . . In my experience I've found they're a waste of time."[3]

However, Cobain later admitted he felt he had to lie about his drug use. Cobain said he did not want to glamorize drugs, maintaining that he only used heroin to ease his stomach pain.

GROWING APART

Nevermind was still near the top of the charts as winter turned to spring in 1992, but Cobain's drug issues threatened Nirvana's future. Novoselic, who had cut back on his drinking for the sake of the band, strongly disapproved of Cobain's drug habits. Even Grohl, who was known as the most laid-back member of Nirvana, was upset by Cobain's downward spiral. Much of what Novoselic and Grohl knew about Cobain's drug problems was based on rumors. Meanwhile, Cobain and Love felt Nirvana's other members were not supportive enough.

To make matters worse, Cobain and Love had moved to Los Angeles, California, far away from the other band members. The tension remained as the band set out on a European tour that summer.

Near Breakup

Rumors persisted that Nirvana might break up in 1992 due to Cobain's heroin addiction. However, when the band came closest to breaking up, the reason had nothing to do with drugs. After *Nevermind* began making lots of money, the band agreed Cobain should take a higher percentage of the band's royalties because he wrote most of the music and was the face of the band. However, the trio fiercely disagreed how the money should be split. Eventually, Cobain took 75 percent. "At the time, I was ready to . . . quit the band over it," Cobain said.[4]

Vanity Fair

While pregnant, Love had agreed to do an interview with *Vanity Fair*. She assumed the magazine wanted to write a positive story. Instead, the article, published in September, savaged her. Among other things, the story claimed that Love used heroin throughout her pregnancy. Although Love disputed the claim and other details within the story, many people believed what was written.

The reaction devastated the young couple. It also came at a terrible time. Cobain had either been taking heroin or a painkilling substitute for most of Love's pregnancy. On August 4, realizing his $400-a-day habit had gone too far, he checked into a hospital for detoxification. A distraught Love soon checked into the same hospital. She was afraid the stress might lead her to take drugs. It was there, on August 18, 1992, that Frances Bean Cobain was born.

In just a few months, Cobain had grown from an unknown musician from Aberdeen to a cultural icon. He was already weary of the fame his new standing had brought him. The attention that came with the *Vanity Fair* story was the worst yet. For the first time, Cobain and Love became the targets of high-profile negative press.

▲ COBAIN HOLDS HIS DAUGHTER, FRANCES BEAN.

Frances Bean was born without any problems, but the nightmare continued. The *Vanity Fair* article triggered the Department of Children's Services to investigate Cobain and Love. Soon after Frances Bean was born, she was taken away. "It was just so humiliating, and it just felt like so many powerful people were out to get us that it seemed hopeless," Cobain said.[5]

The *Vanity Fair* article had caused a stir, but few people knew of Cobain and Love's personal struggle in its aftermath. Likewise, few knew that Frances Bean had been taken away from her parents. That stress made it hard for Cobain to perform with Nirvana, which was still at the peak of its popularity. On August 30, the band was scheduled to headline the famous Reading Festival in England. The strain over losing their daughter became so unbearable that Cobain and Love briefly considered taking their own lives. Instead, they decided to fight for their daughter.

7

BACK TO BASICS

The week of the Reading Festival, British newspapers had been speculating about rumors of Nirvana breaking up and about Cobain's health problems. When it was finally time for Nirvana to play, Cobain was ready. He came on stage wearing a hospital gown and sitting in a wheelchair, mocking the sensational headlines. He followed by playing an emotional show. Many fans regard that Reading performance as Nirvana's finest.

▶ DESPITE STRUGGLES IN HIS PERSONAL LIFE, COBAIN PERFORMED AT THE 1992 READING MUSIC FESTIVAL.

VIDEO MUSIC AWARDS

Each fall, MTV holds its Video Music Awards (VMAs). It is one of the biggest events of the year in popular music. In 1992, Nirvana was not only nominated for two awards, but the band was also invited to perform at the awards show on September 8.

MTV wanted the band to play "Smells Like Teen Spirit." But Nirvana had been under the impression that it could pick which song to perform. So, rather than play its biggest hit, Nirvana decided a few hours before the show to play nothing at all, which would have been a huge blow to the awards show. However, the band realized some of their friends at MTV could be fired or the influential station could get payback by cutting ties with other DGC bands. In a compromise, Nirvana agreed to play "Lithium," another single off *Nevermind*.

However, Nirvana was not a band that liked to bow to authority. So when Cobain took the stage, he began playing an unreleased song called "Rape Me." Then, before shocked MTV executives could pull the plug on the performance, he switched into "Lithium." The memorable performance ended with Novoselic tossing his bass into the air only to have it bonk

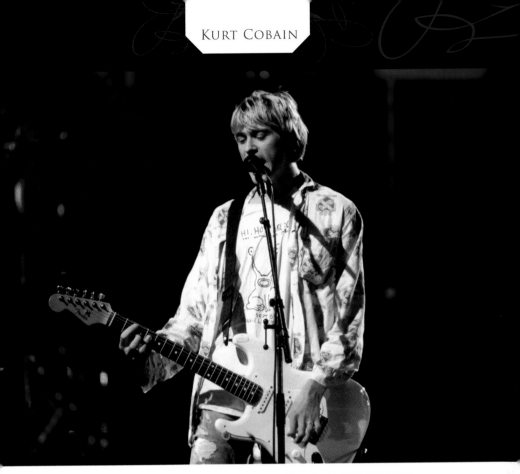

▲ AFTER MUCH BACK AND FORTH, NIRVANA PERFORMED AT THE 1992 MTV VMAS.

him on the head, followed by Cobain throwing his guitar and knocking down a stack of amps. Nirvana collected both awards it was nominated for that night. One was for Best Alternative Video, and the other was for Best New Artist.

Although Nirvana had helped start the mainstream grunge movement nearly a year earlier, their real breakthrough came after the 1992 VMAs. Nirvana's high-profile performance and acceptance speech served as a reminder to fans what the band was all about. Nirvana continued building on its momentum and its reputation. After the VMAs, the band headed to the Pacific Northwest to play two benefit shows. The profits from those shows went to groups fighting a censorship law.

Cobain was still deeply affected by the *Vanity Fair* story and the way people had treated him and Love in its aftermath. But the band had regained some of its intimacy as Novoselic and Grohl learned more about what Cobain and Love had been through. And before long, the struggle to regain custody of Frances Bean finally ended.

FINALLY A FATHER

The process of regaining custody of Frances Bean was a challenging one, but after approximately one month, Cobain

Unauthorized Bio

Fame had brought plenty of unwanted attention to Cobain's personal life. In 1992, he learned two British writers were planning to write a tell-all biography about Nirvana. Cobain worried the book might jeopardize his custody of Frances Bean. In October, an emotional Cobain tried calling the writers to get them to stop. He left nine back-to-back voice messages on the writers' answering machines, ranging in tone from desperate to threatening.

In response, Nirvana decided to issue its own official biography, *Come As You Are: The Story of Nirvana*, in 1993. *Rolling Stone* writer Michael Azerrad wrote the biogra-

▲ COBAIN AND LOVE WERE THRILLED TO FINALLY GET THEIR DAUGHTER BACK IN 1992.

and Love got their daughter back. It was a life-changing moment for Cobain. He and Love still lived in fear of losing their daughter again. They had to constantly prove to the government that they were good parents and not doing drugs. But with Frances Bean in his life, Cobain found it easier to stay clean. "I knew that when I had a child, I'd be overwhelmed and it's true," he told the *Los Angeles Times* in September. "I can't tell you how much my attitude has changed since we've got Frances. Holding my baby is the best drug in the world."[1]

That positive attitude also translated to his music career. Cobain later spoke about his fans:

I don't have as many judgments about them as I used to. . . . I've come to terms about why they're there and why we're here. It doesn't bother me anymore to see this Neanderthal with a mustache, out of his mind, drunk, singing along to "Sliver." That blows my mind now.[2]

Nirvana closed out the year by releasing *Incesticide* on December 15. It was a lightly promoted album featuring rare recordings from before Nirvana was famous.

The fall of 1992 had helped reestablish Nirvana as one of the most popular bands of the era. The year 1993 began with two big shows in Brazil followed by a month-long break. Cobain stayed in the headlines, though.

In February, *The Advocate*, a national gay- and

Incesticide

By late 1992, bootlegged copies of Nirvana recordings were becoming more common. To combat the phenomenon, the band released *Incesticide*. The eclectic mix of songs showed off Nirvana's various influences, from heavy grunge songs such as "Stain" to the catchy "Sliver," a song about a child wanting to leave his grandparents' house. Knowing the album would not have the same mainstream appeal as *Nevermind*, DGC decided not to promote it too heavily. Reviews were mixed, and sales paled in comparison to *Nevermind*, but *Incesticide* proved influential on the underground grunge scene.

lesbian-interest magazine, ran an in-depth interview with Cobain. The singer had long been a supporter of gay rights. Doing the interview with the publication encouraged many Nirvana fans to pick up the magazine and learn more about its cause. Cobain told *The Advocate* he was "gay in spirit."[3] Finally, in mid-February, Nirvana was ready to record its anticipated third album.

IN UTERO

After *Nevermind*, music fans were anxious to see how Nirvana would follow up its popular album. Cobain and Nirvana had already influenced the future of rock music. Cobain had long admired the Beatles, and particularly the band's visionary front man John Lennon. Nirvana's follow-up album would help determine if Nirvana was on its way to following the Beatles by becoming one of the most famous bands of all time. However, Cobain had always wanted to be successful but had mixed feelings about his fame. Some people thought Nirvana might sabotage its third album to alienate all the mainstream fans who embraced the band after *Nevermind*. Before settling on the album's name, Cobain wanted to call it *Verse Chorus Verse*—a reference to the formula he felt his music followed.

▲ AFTER A BUSY YEAR, THE MEMBERS OF NIRVANA WERE READY FOR A CHANGE OF PACE WHEN THEY DECIDED TO START RECORDING ANOTHER ALBUM.

By the time Nirvana was ready to record another album, Cobain had decided that *Nevermind* was overproduced, which he did not like. Cobain wanted to go back to basics for Nirvana's third album. So Nirvana went to producer Steve Albini, who had lots of experience recording other alternative rock bands. Albini also had a reputation for following the punk rock philosophy of keeping things simple.

His recordings sounded more like a live performance than something mixed in a studio.

The band joined Albini at Pachyderm Studio in Cannon Falls, Minnesota. They stayed there for two weeks, doing most of the recording in six days. Both sides remember the process as being efficient and enjoyable. Albini said,

> *I try to make it like day-to-day life. . . . get up in the morning and have breakfast, go to the studio, work, play, set Dave Grohl on fire, then go back to the house to eat dinner and watch wildlife videos.*[4]

Once the album was recorded, rumors were flying that DGC would not approve it. Ultimately, after even Cobain found some songs to be a little too unpolished, *In Utero* was remixed and released in September 1993.

———•◆•———

8

FADING AWAY

On March 23, 1993, the Department of Children's Services announced it was no longer supervising Cobain and Love's parenting skills. This was great news for the couple. However, it also meant they had one less check on their sobriety. Cobain soon began using drugs again. In May, Love brought Cobain back from a heroin overdose by injecting him with another illegal drug. His drug use continued through the summer.

In Utero came out in September, and Nirvana embarked on a US tour soon after. Cobain

▸ BY 1993, COBAIN'S ADDICTION WAS GETTING WORSE, AND HE WAS BECOMING BORED WITH NIRVANA'S MUSIC.

reportedly detoxed prior to the tour. Friends remember Cobain going through periods of happiness and withdrawn sadness throughout the tour. The band was playing some of its best shows. However, Cobain seemed to be growing increasingly bored with Nirvana's music.

A NEW SOUND

Signs of boredom were beginning to show in Nirvana. In the fall of 1993, Cobain told a *Rolling Stone* reporter that Nirvana's future might be limited.

I hate to actually even say it, but I can't see this band lasting more than a couple more albums, unless we really work hard on experimenting. When the same people are together doing the same

In Utero

After Nirvana made it big with the polished recordings on *Nevermind*, the band was determined to get back to its simpler, punk rock roots with *In Utero*. The album showcases Nirvana's varying styles, featuring few recording tricks and sounding more like a live performance. *In Utero* helped Nirvana regain credibility among the hard-core alternative rock fans who felt the band had sold out with *Nevermind*.

The band did not expect the rawer *In Utero* to match *Nevermind's* success, but the album nonetheless debuted on the US charts at Number 1. *In Utero* was generally well received by critics. *Rolling Stone* magazine gave it 4.5 out of 5 stars, with the reviewer saying: "*In Utero* is a lot of things—brilliant, corrosive, enraged, and thoughtful, most of *job, they're limited. . . . I don't want to put out another record that sounds like the last three records.*[2]

In November, the band went on *MTV Unplugged*, a TV show in which bands play an acoustic set in front of a live audience. The show first aired in December. It was one of Nirvana's most famous performances. Cobain talked openly with the crowd between quiet, emotional songs. In addition to Nirvana's own music, the band covered songs from bands they liked. The session showed a different side of Nirvana and was well received by critics. In November 1994, the performance was released as an album, *MTV Unplugged in New York*.

With this shift in style, Cobain followed in the footsteps of one of his biggest influences, John Lennon. One of the reasons many people admire Lennon is because of his growth as a musician. His music evolved in each of the Beatles' albums throughout the 1960s. With performances such as the one for *MTV Unplugged*, people began to recognize Cobain as a more versatile musician. Cobain also had other ideas for projects he wanted to work on. He was particularly interested in working with R.E.M.'s Michael Stipe, an artist

NIRVANA

UNPLUGGED

▲ NIRVANA BROKE FROM ITS TRADITIONAL SOUND WITH
ITS ACOUSTIC *MTV UNPLUGGED* PERFORMANCE.

he admired. However, Nirvana continued sticking
to its heavier grunge music on tours.

TROUBLE IN EUROPE
Nirvana's US tour ended in Seattle on January 8,
1994. A few weeks later, on February 2, the
band left for a 38-show European tour. The
shows started out well. But Cobain soon grew

tired from the travel and began losing his voice. On March 1, Nirvana was playing a show in Munich, Germany, when Cobain's voice finally gave out. He was suffering from severe laryngitis and bronchitis, so after 15 shows the tour was postponed.

Not feeling well enough to fly home to Seattle, where he and his family were living, Cobain flew to Rome. Love and Frances Bean met him there one day later. The next morning, Love found Cobain unconscious. He had taken approximately 50 pills along with drinking champagne the night before. Love rushed him to the hospital. Approximately 20 hours later, he regained consciousness. The incident was initially called an accident. However, a suicide note revealed that Cobain had been attempting to kill himself.

LOST AT HOME

Things did not get much better upon Cobain's return to Seattle. Though few knew it had been a suicide attempt, the incident in Rome had been widely reported on. Cobain's drug problems were growing worse. Those close to Cobain became concerned. They held an intervention to convince him to go to rehab. At the intervention,

▲ COBAIN'S BANDMATES WERE CONCERNED ABOUT HIS ESCALATING DRUG PROBLEM.

Novoselic told Cobain he would break up the band if Cobain did not seek help.

Love threatened to leave him. She was preparing for a trip to Los Angeles to promote Hole's new album. Love was concerned the publicity from the Rome incident could lead to Frances Bean being taken away again. She begged Cobain to join her in Los Angeles, where he could go to rehab while she worked. Cobain listened, but he did not believe he had a drug problem. He stayed in Seattle as Love and Frances Bean went to California.

A few days later, Cobain told his friend Dylan Carlson that people had been trespassing at his house and asked Carlson to buy him a gun. Cobain's guns had been taken away after a domestic dispute with Love a few days earlier. Carlson, not knowing about the suicide attempt in Rome, did not think twice and bought Cobain the gun.

Finally, Cobain agreed to fly down to Los Angeles for rehab. On April 1, after two days in rehab, he called Love. She remembered the conversation in a 1994 *Rolling Stone* interview:

> *He said, "Courtney, no matter what happens, I want you to know that you made a really good record."... I said "Well, what do you mean?" And he said, "Just remember, no matter what, I love you."*[3]

She would never speak to him again.

That evening, Cobain stepped outside of the rehab facility for a cigarette and never came back. Before long, he was back in Seattle. Neighbors reported seeing Cobain over the next couple days, but Love could not reach him. On April 3, she and DGC hired a private investigator to find him. Cobain's mother filed a missing-person's report one day later. Finally, on April 8, someone found him.

———•◆•———

9

STILL BURNING

At approximately 8:40 a.m. on April 8, 1994, an electrician arrived at Cobain and Love's Seattle home to install a security system. When nobody answered the door, the electrician began walking around the house. He eventually reached the greenhouse above the garage. Peering through the window, he saw what he thought was a mannequin lying on the floor. Then he saw a 20-gauge shotgun on the body's chest and a pool of blood by its ear. It was later confirmed that the body was Cobain. Medical examiners determined

▶ COBAIN'S BODY WAS FOUND AT HIS HOME IN SEATTLE ON APRIL 8, 1994.

he had taken a lethal dose of heroin before shooting himself in the head approximately three days earlier. He was 27 years old.

News of Cobain's suicide spread quickly. After the electrician called the police, he called a coworker. That coworker called local radio station KXRX-FM with the electrician's information. The medical examiners did not immediately identify the body, but after the incident in Rome, people seemed to know the rumors were true.

A handful of fans began showing up at Cobain's house. They were joined by an even

▲ COBAIN'S HOUSE IN SEATTLE

bigger group of journalists. MTV, which had been the catalyst for Nirvana's influential rise into the mainstream, took the lead in covering the news. The network interrupted its regular programming with episodes of Nirvana's *Unplugged* performance. It featured regular news updates from a reporter in Seattle and MTV News anchor Kurt Loder. *Time* magazine compared the coverage of Cobain's death to the

1963 assassination of President John F. Kennedy, "with a somber Kurt Loder playing the Walter Cronkite role," referring to the famous news anchor of an earlier generation.[1] Two Seattle radio stations followed suit, abandoning their regular programming to play Nirvana songs all weekend.

MEMORIALS

Cobain's fans were devastated. Two days later, on Sunday, April 10, more than 5,000 fans showed up for a candlelight vigil at a park near the Space Needle in Seattle. Cobain's family and close friends gathered at a nearby church for a private memorial. Several people spoke at the public memorial, including a minister, a grief counselor, and local disc jockeys. The crowd heard taped messages recorded by both Novoselic and Love.

Love's six-minute recording displayed a range of emotions. Clearly crying throughout, Love expressed anger, sadness, confusion, and disbelief as she read excerpts of Cobain's suicide note.

Courtney and Frances

Hole's new album, *Live This*, was released to good reviews on April 12, 1994. Love and Hole remained popular for much of the 1990s. She also had some success as an actress. However, her life remained tumultuous following Cobain's death. Drug problems continued to plague her, resulting in Frances Bean again being taken away for a time. Later in life, Love continued expressing anger toward Cobain for committing suicide. Frances Bean turned 18 in 2010 but has remained largely out of the public eye.

▲ THOUSANDS OF FANS MET TO MOURN COBAIN AS A GROUP AT A MEMORIAL SERVICE IN SEATTLE.

The crowd mirrored her conflicted emotions, even swearing at Cobain when she directed them to.

Cobain's suicide note offered some insights into his decision to kill himself. He discussed the guilt he felt about "faking it."[2] He wrote, "I haven't felt the excitement of listening to as well as creating music along with really writing something for two years now. . . . I feel guilty beyond words about these things."[3]

Of his fans, Cobain said: "On our last three tours I had a much better appreciation of all the people I know personally and the fans of our music."[4] Ultimately, he said there was simply a sadness he could not rid himself of. He wrote,

I had it good—very good—and I'm grateful. But since the age of seven, I've become hateful toward all humans in general only because it seems so easy for people to get along and have empathy only because I love and feel for people too much I guess.[5]

DON'T FADE AWAY

Near the end of Cobain's suicide note, he wrote:

Selfish

Many mourners expressed sadness as they celebrated Cobain's life. Others looked at Cobain's decision as self-ish. "He died a coward," a disc jockey from KIRO-FM in Seattle said, "and left a little girl without a father."[7] In addition, some pointed out that Cobain's suicide left the impression that suicide was an acceptable way to deal with problems.

Thank you all from the pit of my burning, nauseous stomach for your letters and concern during the last years. I'm too much of an erratic, moody person and I don't have the passion anymore. So remember, it's better to burn out than to fade away.[6]

Cobain's legacy did not fade away with his life on that April day in 1994. In 1991, his visionary songwriting propelled grunge music into the mainstream. The music on *Nevermind* gave a generation of youth a voice with which to express their angst about the changing world. Nirvana also played a major role in getting major record labels and MTV to pay attention to alternative rock. Even though grunge as a music style was coming to a close at the time of Cobain's death, Nirvana's music proved to be timeless. Respected organizations such as *Rolling Stone* and MTV ranked Nirvana's songs, albums, and music videos as among the greatest of all time.

Alternative rock, meanwhile, evolved into different styles after Cobain's death. Diverse alternative bands such as Oasis, Radiohead, Creed, and Bush rose to popularity in the mid-to-late 1990s. Before *Nevermind*, alternative rock was mostly an underground genre. Neither the Grammy Awards nor the VMAs had categories

"You Know You're Right"

In January 1994, Nirvana had recorded its last studio song, "You Know You're Right." It was a classic Nirvana song, switching between a catchy but subdued melody and loud, grinding noise. Eight years later, the song still had not been released. A bitter legal battle ensued between Love and Cobain's former bandmates, Novoselic and Grohl. Eventually it was decided the song would be included on Nirvana's 2002 greatest hits album titled *Nirvana*.

▲ GROHL WENT ON TO START ANOTHER ALTERNATIVE BAND, THE FOO FIGHTERS, WHICH HAS BEEN HUGELY SUCCESSFUL.

for alternative music before 1991. Today, it is a major mainstream genre, with many bands still owing direct influence to Nirvana.

One of those bands is the Foo Fighters. After Cobain's death, Grohl formed the Foo Fighters and became its lead singer and guitarist. The Foo Fighters became one of the most popular alternative rock bands of the late 1990s and early 2000s. They won five awards at the 2011 Grammy Awards, including Best Rock Song and Best Rock Album. Although Novoselic never made it big again, he also continued playing music.

It is impossible to know what would have come next for Cobain. The actions prior to his suicide note hinted he was interested in experimenting with new kinds of music. Following the success of Nirvana's *Unplugged* performance, perhaps he would have ventured further into acoustic music. Still, in just three studio albums, Cobain influenced rock music forever. Music critics and fans alike can only imagine what he might have accomplished had he continued making music.

———•◆•———

 TIMELINE

1967

Kurt Donald Cobain is born on February 20 in Hoquiam, Washington.

1975

Cobain's parents, Don and Wendy Cobain, divorce.

1984

Buzz Osborne takes Cobain to Seattle to see Black Flag. It is Cobain's first punk rock show.

1988

Cobain, Novoselic, and Dale Crover record a demo in Seattle, putting Cobain's music on tape for the first time.

1988

Nirvana signs with Sub Pop, an independent record label influential in the grunge movement.

1989

Bleach is released in the summer.

1985

Cobain drops out of high school just shy of graduation.

1986

Cobain forms his first band, Fecal Matter.

1987

Cobain and Chris Novoselic bring in drummer Aaron Burckhard, creating the beginnings of Nirvana.

1989

Cobain meets Courtney Love at a rock concert.

1991

Nirvana leaves Sub Pop in the winter and signs with DGC Records, a major label.

1991

"Smells Like Teen Spirit" is released as a single on September 10.

TIMELINE

1991

Nevermind is released on September 24. It reaches gold status within three weeks.

1991

MTV adds "Smells Like Teen Spirit" to its regular music video rotation on October 14.

1992

Cobain marries Love in Hawaii during a small ceremony on February 24.

1993

Nirvana releases its fourth album, *In Utero*, in October.

1993

In November, Nirvana performs an acoustic set on *MTV Unplugged*, which is released as an album in 1994.

1994

In March, Love finds Cobain unconscious at a hotel room in Rome, Italy. It is later revealed to be a suicide attempt.

1992

A *Vanity Fair* profile accuses Love of taking heroin during her pregnancy. It devastates the couple.

1992

Frances Bean Cobain is born on August 18.

1992

Nirvana's third album, *Incesticide*, is released in December. It is a collection of rare recordings.

1994

On April 8, an electrician finds Cobain's body.

1999

MTV named "Smells Like Teen Spirit" the third best music video ever.

2002

Nirvana's greatest hits album is released, which includes the new song "You Know You're Right."

 Quick Facts

DATE OF BIRTH
February 20, 1967

PLACE OF BIRTH
Hoquiam, Washington

DATE OF DEATH
April 5, 1994

PLACE OF DEATH
Seattle, Washington

PARENTS
Don and Wendy Cobain

MARRIAGE
Courtney Love (1992)

CHILDREN
Frances Bean Cobain

CAREER HIGHLIGHTS
Studio Albums
Bleach (1989)
Nevermind (1991)
In Utero (1993)

Other Albums
Incesticide (1992)
MTV Unplugged in New York (1994)
From the Muddy Banks of the Wishkah (1996)
Live at Reading (2009)

QUOTE
"The best times were right when *Nevermind* was coming out and we went on that American tour where we were playing clubs. . . . There was this massive feeling in the air, this vibe of energy. Something really special was happening."—*Kurt Cobain*

GLOSSARY

acoustic
Music that is not electronically amplified.

bootlegged
Illegally recorded music.

catalyst
Something that brings change.

cover band
A band that plays the music of another band.

detoxification
The process of withdrawing drugs or alcohol out of someone's body.

festival
A large outdoor concert featuring several bands.

genre
A category of music, such as country or alternative rock.

headliner
The main act in a rock concert.

hook
A catchy part of a song that draws listeners in and is easily remembered.

macho
Stereotypically masculine.

mixtape
A collection of different songs recorded onto a cassette tape.

producer
> Someone who oversees or provides money for a play, television show, movie, or album.

punk
> An aggressive style of rock music that began during the 1970s; the music was about being loud and edgy.

record label
> A company that manages a band's music, particularly in regards to producing, manufacturing, distributing, and marketing albums.

rehab
> Short for rehabilitation; an effort to overcome an addiction to drugs or alcohol.

remixed
> Altered sounds on a piece of music.

royalties
> Money given to an artist based on a percentage of sales.

set
> The group of songs played by a band at a performance.

single
> An individual song released by a band for play on the radio.

studio album
> An album made up of tracks recorded in a studio.

ADDITIONAL RESOURCES

SELECTED BIBLIOGRAPHY

Azerrad, Michael. *Come As You Are: The Story of Nirvana*. New York: Broadway Books, 1993. Print.

Azerrad, Michael. "Nirvana: Inside the Heart and Mind of Kurt Cobain." *Rolling Stone* 16 Apr. 1992: 36–41, 96–97. Print.

Cross, Charles R. *Heavier Than Heaven: A Biography of Kurt Cobain*. New York: Hyperion, 2001. Print.

Sandford, Christopher. *Kurt Cobain*. New York: Carroll & Graf, 1996. Print.

Thompson, Dave. *Never Fade Away: The Kurt Cobain Story*. New York: St. Martin's, 1994. Print.

FURTHER READINGS

Brannigan, Paul. *This Is a Call: The Life and Times of Dave Grohl*. Cambridge, MA: Da Capo, 2011. Print.

Cobain, Kurt. *Journals*. New York: Riverhead Books, 2003. Print.

Cross, Charles R. *Cobain Unseen*. New York: Little, Brown, 2008. Print.

Neely, Kim. *Five Against One: The Pearl Jam Story*. New York: Penguin, 1998. Print.

Yarm, Mark. *Everybody Loves Our Town: An Oral History of Grunge*. New York: Crown Archetype, 2011. Print.

WEB LINKS

To learn more about Kurt Cobain, visit ABDO Publishing Company online at **www.abdopublishing.com**. Web sites about Kurt Cobain are featured on our Book Links page. These links are routinely monitored and updated to provide the most current information available.

FOR MORE INFORMATION

For more information on this subject, contact or visit the following organizations.

Aberdeen Museum of History
111 East Third Street, Aberdeen, Washington 98520
360-533-1976
www.aberdeen-museum.org
The museum highlights the history of Aberdeen, Washington, where Kurt Cobain grew up. The museum's Web site offers information for visitors wishing to conduct a walking tour of places Cobain lived or frequented while living in Aberdeen.

EMP Museum
325 Fifth Avenue North, Seattle, WA 98109
206-770-2700
www.empmuseum.org
The EMP Museum, formerly known as the Experience Music Project, is a museum in the heart of downtown Seattle celebrating popular music. Visitors learn about music through collections of artifacts and interactive exhibits.

SOURCE NOTES

Chapter 1. *Nevermind*

1. David Fricke. "The Rolling Stone Interview: Kurt Cobain." *Rolling Stone* 27 Jan. 1994: 36. *Rolling Stone All Access*. Web. 16 Mar. 2012.

2. "Nirvana: 'Smells Like Teen Spirit.'" *Rolling Stone*. Rolling Stone, 2011. Web. 15 Jan. 2012.

3. Stacey Anderson. "Jon Stewart Talks Nirvana With Krist Novoselic, Dave Grohl and Butch Vig." *Rolling Stone*. Rolling Stone, 26 Sept. 2011. Web. 15 Jan. 2012.

4. Michael Azerrad. "Nirvana: Inside the Heart and Mind of Kurt Cobain." *Rolling Stone*. 16 Apr. 1992. Print. 39.

Chapter 2. *Aberdeen*

1. Michael Azerrad. *Come As You Are: The Story of Nirvana.* New York: Broadway Books, 1993. Print. 14.

2. Ibid. 15.

3. Ibid. 17.

Chapter 3. *Punk Rocker*

1. Michael Azerrad. *Come As You Are: The Story of Nirvana.* New York: Broadway Books, 1993. Print. 32.

2. Mark Yarm. "Commentary: The Roots of Grunge Run Deep." *CNN.com*. Cable News Network, 23 Sept. 2011. Web. 7 Dec. 2011.

3. Krist Novoselic. "Krist Novoselic: We All Owe Something to The Melvins." Seattle Weekly. *Seattle Weekly*, 20 Jan. 2009. Web. 16 Dec. 2011.

4. Christopher Sandford. *Kurt Cobain*. New York: Carroll & Graf, 1996. Print. 53.

5. Michael Azerrad. *Come As You Are: The Story of Nirvana.* New York: Broadway Books, 1993. Print. 33.

Chapter 4. Nirvana Begins

1. Christopher Sandford. *Kurt Cobain.* New York: Carroll & Graf, 1996. Print. 73.

2. Michael Azerrad. *Come As You Are: The Story of Nirvana.* New York: Broadway Books, 1993. Print. 100.

3. David Fricke. "The Tenth Anniversary of Nirvana's Nevermind." *Rolling Stone* 13 Sept. 2001: 76. *Rolling Stone All Access.* Web. 16 Mar. 2012.

4. Dave Thompson. *Never Fade Away: The Kurt Cobain Story.* New York: St. Martin's, 1994. Print. 64.

5. Charles R. Cross. *Heavier Than Heaven: A Biography of Kurt Cobain.* New York: Hyperion, 2001. Print. 124.

6. Michael Azerrad. *Come As You Are: The Story of Nirvana.* New York: Broadway Books, 1993. Print. 115.

7. Ibid. 134–135.

8. Ibid. 158.

Chapter 5. Rock Star

1. Michael Azerrad. *Come As You Are: The Story of Nirvana.* New York: Broadway Books, 1993. Print. 155.

2. David Fricke. "The Rolling Stone Interview: Kurt Cobain." *Rolling Stone* 27 Jan. 1994: 57. *Rolling Stone All Access.* Web. 16 Mar. 2012.

3. Michael Azerrad. "Nirvana: Inside the Heart and Mind of Kurt Cobain." *Rolling Stone* 16 Apr. 1992: 38. *Rolling Stone All Access.* Web. 16 Mar. 2012.

4. James Montgomery. "Nirvana On 'Headbangers Ball': Behind The Ball Gown." *MTV.* Viacom International, 21 Sept. 2011. Web. 16 Dec. 2011.

5. Michael Azerrad. "Nirvana: Inside the Heart and Mind of Kurt Cobain." *Rolling Stone* 16 Apr. 1992: 38. *Rolling Stone All Access.* Web. 16 Mar. 2012.

6. Christopher Sandford. *Kurt Cobain.* New York: Carroll & Graf, 1996. Print. 197.

7. Matt Diehl. "Anarchy in the U.S." *Rolling Stone* 13 Sept. 2001: 83. *Rolling Stone All Access*. Web. 16 Mar. 2012.

8. Michael Azerrad. *Come As You Are: The Story of Nirvana*. New York: Broadway Books, 1993. Print. 194.

Chapter 6. Love and Drugs

1. Michael Azerrad. *Come As You Are: The Story of Nirvana*. New York: Broadway Books, 1993. Print. 169.

2. Ibid. 205.

3. Michael Azerrad. "Nirvana: Inside the Heart and Mind of Kurt Cobain." *Rolling Stone* 16 Apr. 1992: 38. *Rolling Stone All Access*. Web. 16 Mar. 2012.

4. Michael Azerrad. *Come As You Are: The Story of Nirvana*. New York: Broadway Books, 1993. Print. 258.

5. Ibid. 271.

Chapter 7. Back to Basics

1. Robert Hilburn. "Cobain to Fans: Just Say No." Los Angeles Times. *Los Angeles Times*, 11 Sept. 1992. Web. 15 Jan. 2012.

2. David Fricke. "The Rolling Stone Interview: Kurt Cobain." *Rolling Stone* 27 Jan. 1994: 36. *Rolling Stone All Access*. Web. 16 Mar. 2012.

3. Michael Azerrad. *Come As You Are: The Story of Nirvana*. New York: Broadway Books, 1993. Print. 312.

4. Dave Thompson. *Never Fade Away: The Kurt Cobain Story*. New York: St. Martin's, 1994. Print. 142.

Chapter 8. Fading Away

1. David Fricke. "Nirvana *In Utero*." *Rolling Stone*. Rolling Stone, 16 Sept. 1993. Web. 31 Dec. 2011.

2. David Fricke. "The Rolling Stone Interview: Kurt Cobain." *Rolling Stone* 27 Jan. 1994: 36. *Rolling Stone All Access*. Web. 16 Mar. 2012.

3. Neil Strauss and Alec Foege. "The Downward Spiral." *Rolling Stone* June 2, 1994: 36. *Rolling Stone All Access.* Web. 16 Mar. 2012.

Chapter 9. Still Burning
1. Bruce Handy, Lisa McLaughlin, Jeffrey Ressner, and Dave Thompson. "MUSIC: Never Mind." *TIME.* Time, Apr. 18, 1994. Web. 1 Jan. 2012.

2. Michael Azerrad. *Come As You Are: The Story of Nirvana.* New York: Broadway Books, 1993. Print. 348.

3. Ibid. 348.

4. Ibid. 348.

5. Ibid. 349.

6. Ibid. 349.

7. Neil Strauss and Alec Foege. "The Downward Spiral." *Rolling Stone* June 2, 1994: 43. *Rolling Stone All Access.* Web. 16 Mar. 2012.

NDEX

Aberdeen, Washington, 16, 18, 29, 30, 31, 32, 33, 35, 36, 40, 55
"About a Girl," 39
Advocate, the, 74–75
Albini, Steve, 76–77
Azerrad, Michael, 72,

Beatles, 19–20, 75, 81
Bleach, 39, 41, 44, 46, 51
Brown Towel, 34
Burckhard, Aaron, 35, 36, 40, 43

Carlson, Dylan, 84–85
Channing, Chad, 43, 47, 48
Cobain, Don (father), 16, 18, 20–21, 23–24, 26, 32
Cobain, Frances Bean, 65–67, 72–74, 83–84, 90
Cobain, Kimberly (sister), 18, 21
Cobain, Kurt
  art, 20, 34
  childhood, 18–24, 26–29
  chronic pain, 38, 61
  death, 86, 88–95
  drug use, 15, 29, 33–34, 38, 56, 60–64, 78, 83
  education, 29, 32–33
  family, 18–24, 29, 30, 32
  memorials, 90–91
  songwriting, 6, 8, 12, 34, 54, 93

Cobain, Wendy (mother), 16, 18, 20–21, 26, 29, 33–34, 85
"Come As You Are," 12
Crover, Dale, 40, 43

DGC Records, 12–13, 50, 55, 70, 74, 77, 85

Endino, Jack, 40, 42

Fecal Matter, 34
"Floyd the Barber," 38
Foo Fighters, 50, 94–95
Fradenburg, Chuck (uncle), 26

Grohl, Dave, 8, 10, 40, 48, 50, 64, 72, 77, 93, 94
grunge, 9–10, 12–13, 16, 30, 42, 54, 71, 74, 82, 93

hair metal, 9–10, 54
Headbangers Ball, 53
heroin, 38, 61–65, 78, 88
Hole, 58, 60, 84, 90

In Utero, 20, 76–77, 78, 80
Incesticide, 20, 41, 74

Lennon, John, 75, 81
"Lithium," 70
Loder, Kurt, 89–90
Love, Courtney, 58, 60–67, 72–73, 78, 83–85, 86, 88, 90

"Love Buzz," 38, 44
Lukin, Matt, 29, 34

Marander, Tracy, 36, 39
Melvins, 29, 30, 35, 40, 43
MTV, 13, 15, 53, 70, 89, 93
MTV Music Video Awards, 70
MTV Unplugged, 81
murder theories, 88

Nevermind, 8, 10, 12–15, 42,
    44, 50–57, 62, 64, 70, 74,
    75–76, 80, 93
Nirvana
    albums. *See names of*
        individual albums
    awards, 70–71
    biography, 72
    breakup rumors, 55, 64
    criticism of, 45, 74, 80,
        81
    fan base, 13, 21, 47, 55, 56,
        68, 72, 74–75, 80, 88, 90,
        92
    name, 42
    performances, 13, 38, 45, 47,
        55–56, 68, 70–71, 74, 81
    songs. *See names of individual*
        songs
    tours, 45–47, 48, 56, 78, 80,
        82–83

Novoselic, Chris, 10, 12, 30,
    34–35, 36, 38–39, 40, 42, 47,
    48, 50, 53, 63–64, 70–71, 72,
    84, 90, 93, 95

Osborne, Buzz, 29, 30, 39

Pavitt, Bruce, 42
Pearl Jam, 10, 14, 62
Pixies, 50
Poneman, Jonathan, 42
punk rock, 10, 14, 29–30, 32,
    39, 50, 51, 53, 58, 76, 80

"Rape Me," 70
Reading Festival, 67, 68
Red Hot Chili Peppers, 14, 62
R.E.M., 81
Rolling Stone, 15, 53, 55, 63, 72,
    80, 85, 93

Saturday Night Live, 13, 57, 62
Seattle, Washington, 10, 16, 30,
    40, 44, 82–85, 86, 89–90, 92
"Sliver," 74
"Smells Like Teen Spirit," 6, 8,
    12–13, 15, 53, 70
Sonic Youth, 45, 52
"Stain," 74
Sub Pop, 42, 48, 50–51

Vanity Fair, 65–67, 72
Vig, Butch, 51

ABOUT THE AUTHOR

Chrös McDougall is a writer and editor who specializes
in sports and history subjects. Although a generation late,
McDougall grew up listening to Nirvana, reading books about
Kurt Cobain, and playing the main riff for "Come as You Are"
on his guitar. Unfortunately, that riff was all he could play. He
lives in Minnesota's Twin Cities with his wife.

PHOTO CREDITS

Frank Micelotta/Getty Images, cover, 3, 71; Photofest, 7,
11, 49, 57, 76, 84; Chris Gardner/AP Images, 9; John S.
Sfondilias/Shutterstock Images, 17; Press Association/AP
Images, 19, 54, 98; Seth Poppel/Yearbook Library, 23, 25,
28, 97 (top); Roger Sargent/Rex Features/Everett Collection,
27; David Corio/Redferns/Getty Images, 31; Mick Hutson/
Redferns/Getty Images, 35, 69; Kevin Mazur/WireImage/
Getty Images, 37; Dana Nalbandian/WireImage/Getty Images,
41; Charles Peterson/AP Images, 43, 96; Jeff Davy/Retna/
Photoshot/Everett Collection, 46; Dave Lewis/Rex Features/
Everett Collection, 59; DGC/Photofest, 61; Stephen Sweet/
Rex USA/Everett Collection, 66, 99 (top); Terry McGinnis/
WireImage/Getty Images, 73, 97 (bottom); AP Images, 79;
PRNewsFoto/Universal Music Enterprises/AP Images, 82;
Robert Sorbo/AP Images, 87, 99 (bottom); Therese Frare/AFP/
Getty Images, 89, 91; Matt Sayles/AP Images, 94